"Don't Ma

Six Week Study Guide

Ginger Hubbard

Shepherd Press
Wapwallopen, PA

"Don't Make Me Count to Three!" Six Week Study Guide
© 2012 by Ginger Hubbard

ISBN
Paperback ISBN: 9781936908547
Mobi ISBN: 9780972304672
ePub ISBN: 9780981540085

All Scripture quotations are from the Holy Bible, New International Version
(NIV), ©The International Bible Society 1960, 1972, 1976, 1984.

First printing, 2012

Go to: http://www.shepherdpress.com/ebooks

Special thanks to Toma Knight, Kim Young and Sarah Everett
For your insights and help.

Introduction

Before you settle alone on your couch with a cup of coffee or gather with friends to venture into this study, I ask that you ponder your motives for doing so. Are you hoping that upon completion you will have acquired all the knowledge necessary to achieve perfect parenting skills? Are you eager for a plan of action that will transform your children into obedient, respectful angels who never sass and joyfully clean their rooms after one request? Are you expecting that this course of study is the answer to a peaceful home where no conflicts reside? If you answered 'yes' to any of these questions, I hate to be the bearer of bad news, but you have signed up for the wrong study. Pour out your coffee, return your book and demand a refund.

There is no such thing as perfect parenting. There are no parenting books, charts or three step plans that hold the key to transforming us into flawless parents or our offspring into perfect children. There is, however, a Savior who forgives our mistakes, covers our imperfections, and deems us faultless when we admit our inadequacies and cry out to Him for atonement and help.

Striving to be the perfect parent may seem a noble endeavor, but it plants our feet on the sinking sand of self-reliance. Only God has the power to truly reach the hearts of our children. We may work hard to say and do all the right things. We may faithfully implement disciplinary strategies of those who have gone before us, claiming victory in what seems to be tried and true methods.

However, it is not until we admit that our efforts are worthless and acknowledge God as the great power source for a transformed life, that we are able to give up the daily defeat of self-reliance and live in the hope and peace that God is working in us, through us, and even without us. Our efforts are weak at best. We must fully rely on the grace and righteousness of God for the character development, outcome and very souls of our children.

In realizing and accepting this simple truth, we are able to unload the heavy burden of self-dependency and rest assured that when it comes to raising our children God's work will be carried out to completion. Holding fast to this realization also enables us to resist the temptation of pride when our children turn out well or the despairing feeling of defeat when they don't.

On the flip side, we also have a commanded responsibility to raise our children in the discipline and instruction of the Lord. In his Word, God has given us valuable nuggets of wisdom for carrying out this task. The key is found in being active in executing God's command to rightly parent while embracing the perspective that nothing we do is right apart from the atonement of Christ.

It is my desire that this study encourages parents to unearth nuggets of wisdom and sow them into the hearts of their children, while also learning to let go of the fruitless bondage of self-dependency. We do this by totally depending on God. Through this dependency, we act, but also rest in the freedom of knowing it is only by the grace of God that our actions produce fruit.

In light of this line of thinking I ask that you rethink the earlier questions and, once again, ponder your motives for venturing into this study. Are you hopeful that upon completion you will have acquired a deeper dependency on God for parenting? Are you eager for the transformation of your own heart and mind, from the tendency to try to control your children, into the tendency to trust God with your children? Are you expectant that this course of study will enhance your understanding that as long as Jesus is central, a home can be peaceful even when conflicts reside? If you answered 'yes' to these questions, I have good news for you. You have signed up for the right study. Pour that cup of coffee, settle in and join the journey!

Week One

Being a mom is one of the most challenging, rewarding, exhausting, exhilarating, daunting, and satisfying responsibilities a woman can face. Depending on attitudes, moods and responses, there are days it can make us and days it can break us. It triggers every emotion known to women, both good and bad. However, motherhood is truly one of the greatest blessings granted. With this great blessing comes great responsibility to love, train, encourage, correct, nurture and discipline the one(s) with whom we have been blessed. In all of these responsibilities the end goal should be to point our children to Christ. Any efforts made with disregard to this are efforts made in vain. Therefore, we must discipline ourselves to seek God in our own lives in order to be better equipped to train our children to do the same.

Reading

Chapter One: The High Calling of Motherhood

Chapter Two: Defining Discipline

Appendix A

Memorization

Matthew 22:37-38

Jesus replied: "Love the Lord your God with all your heart and with all your soul and with all your mind. This is the first and greatest commandment.

Questions: Chapter One

1. What is your greatest challenge as a mom?

2. List two or three reasons a mom might struggle with pride.

    (1)

    (2)

    (3)

3. Write or paraphrase the following verses:

    (1) Proverbs 8:13:

    (2) Proverbs 13:10:

    (3) Proverbs 16:18:

4. List the characteristics of a noble wife found in Proverbs 31:10-31. How might her tasks compare with those of a modern day mom?

5. According to 1 Peter 5:8, why should we be self-controlled and alert? How might being self-controlled and alert apply in parenting?

6. King Solomon constantly warned his sons to avoid bad counsel and encouraged them to follow godly counsel. What specific warning did he give his son in Proverbs 1:10? What specific encouragement did he give his son in Proverbs 19:20?

7. Look up Romans 15:4. What do we gain from reading Scripture? How does this verse encourage you as a parent?

8. Read Ephesians 6:2-3. What does God promise a child who chooses to submit to parental authority?

9. Why, as Psalm 119:11 says, is it important for us and our children to hide God's Word in our hearts?

10. Some parents view raising children as a frightening task full of uncertainties. How might parents find encouragement and confidence through Joshua 1:9?

11. Read Proverbs 14:1. What are some ways a wise woman might build her house? What are some ways a foolish woman might tear hers down?

12. Tedd Tripp says, "The fear of the Lord is a response to his holiness and his hatred of wickedness." Based on the following references, what blessings come from fearing the Lord?

    (a) Psalm 34:7:

    (b) Psalm 111:10:

    (c) Psalm 128:1-2:

    (d) Psalm 145:19:

    (e) Proverbs 10:27:

    (f) Proverbs 22:4:

13. Total dependence on the wisdom of God is key to good parenting. When we seek the Lord, depending on his power and strength to sustain us, what is he able to do according to Ephesians 3:20?

14. What, according to 2 Corinthians 5:14-15, compels us to love God and teach our children to love God?

15. Read 2 Timothy 1:5. Who obviously had a profound spiritual influence in Timothy's life? How does this encourage you?

Questions: Chapter Two

1. While appropriate outward behavior has its benefits, what should be our primary focus in training our children in righteousness?

2. Because many parents today have a distorted view of discipline, they avoid it altogether. List a few common misconceptions of discipline.

3. God has placed parents as the authority over their children. Record the implications in terms of parental authority found in the verses below.

   • Genesis 18:19

   • Proverbs 1:8-9

   • Proverbs 4:1-2

   • Proverbs 22:6

   • Colossians 3:20-21

   • 1 Thessalonians 2:11-12

4. Biblical discipline involves _____, the _____, and _____.

5. According to Ephesians 6:4, how are we to avoid exasperating our children?

6. What motive should a child have for obeying his parents?

7. How might you encourage your child toward a right motive in obeying?

8. What is said about the Proverbs 31 woman regarding her tongue?

9. Where, in light of Proverbs 2:6 and James 1:5, does wisdom come from?

10. List three biblical truths that help us understand our sin nature?

    (1)

    (2)

    (3)

11. What are the dangers of focusing only on outward behavior?

12. What are the benefits of focusing on the heart?

13. According to Paul's words in Romans 1:16-17, why should we be quick to teach our children from a gospel-oriented perspective?

14. In Matthew 19:14-15, how did Jesus treat children? In what way should this influence our perspective of children?

Application

1. What did you learn most from chapters one and two?

2. How did you apply this to your life this week?

3. What were the results?

Discussion Notes:

Prayer Requests:

Week Two

It is part of our human nature to judge a book by the cover. We tend to gauge what is on the inside by what we see on the outside. If the outside of the cup is clean, the inside must be clean as well. All too often, we measure our own spiritual condition and the spiritual condition of our children by the manifestations of outward behavior. When we lay our heads down at night and reflect on good deeds we have done, we feel good about ourselves. When reflection reveals wrong-doing, we feel badly. It's the same with our children. When the day resulted in a characterization of obedience and good attitudes on their parts, we feel good about them. When they battled us constantly, rebelling in every way, we don't. Certainly, outward behavior can be an indicator of a spiritual condition, but it can also be a stumbling block, causing us to miss God's purposes for the heart. God is always most concerned with the heart. If we are to be more like Him, we must be too.

Reading

Chapter Three: Drawing Out Issues of the Heart

Chapter Four: Training Children in Righteousness

Memorization

James 1:5

If any of you lacks wisdom, you should ask God, who gives generously to all without finding fault, and it will be given to you.

Questions: Chapter Three

1. What two abilities are beneficial for effective communication?

(1)

(2)

2. Outward behaviors are manifestations of what?

3. What wisdom can be gained from the following verses in relation to parents communicating with their children?

   Proverbs 18:2

   Proverbs 18:13

4. In what ways do children benefit from learning how to recognize and understand their own heart-motives?

5. List three skills parents should learn for effective heart-probing.

   (1)

   (2)

   (3)

6. Throughout Scripture, how did Jesus cause people to evaluate their own hearts through questions?

7. In reference to the scenario on page 42, answer the following questions.

   (1) What was the reason Josh could not answer the "why" questions?

   (2) At first, what was mom missing in this situation?

   (3) What heart issues were revealed through good questions?

8. What three goals are parents looking to accomplish through the use of heart-probing questions?

   (1)

   (2)

   (3)

9. What three issues might we walk our children through when probing their hearts?

> (1)

> (2)

> (3)

10. How do the promises and blessings found in Psalm 34:8-11 encourage you to train your children in the ways of the Lord?

11. Consider a time when you were talking to someone who obviously wasn't paying attention. How did this make you feel? What actions or non-actions revealed their lack of interest? Are you guilty of similar actions or non-actions when your child is talking? If so, what can you do to be more attentive?

12. Wisdom from the Lord is what we need in parenting. Look up Proverbs 2:1-6 and list the actions we must take in order to attain wisdom.

13. According to James 3:13-18, what does worldly wisdom produce? What does godly wisdom produce?

14. In 2 Timothy 3:16, what did Paul say God's Word is useful for?

15. Take a moment to pray for your children, using Paul's prayer in Ephesians 3:16-19 as your guide.

Questions: Chapter Four

1. According to Ephesians 4:22-24, what are we to put off? What are we to put on? How does this process apply to training children in righteousness?

2. In the example given on page 48, what was the "way of escape"?

3. How do children learn to biblically govern their own behavior?

4. Answer the following questions regarding the scenario of Wesley aggravating his sister.

    (1) What had mom failed to do in the beginning?

    (2) What steps did she take in order to train more thoroughly and more productively?

    (3) How did her efforts benefit her children?

5. Explain the value of role-playing.

6. What verses might you apply to "tattling"?

7. Today's children are bombarded with unrighteous teachings from a culture that has "lost all sensitivity and given itself to sensuality" (Ephesians 4:19). The closer we move toward end times, the more intense ungodly influences will become. List the ungodly characteristics of people as described by Paul in 2 Timothy 3:1-5.

8. Our goal in training our children in righteousness is to point them to their need for Christ. According to Deuteronomy 6:6-7, when and where are we to talk to our children about the ways of the Lord?

9. What, as stated in Colossians 3:16, are we to let dwell in us richly as we teach and admonish?

10. Read Psalm 119:130. Where should our words come from in order that they might bring forth light?

11. According to Romans 10:17, what fruit will scripture bear in your family's life?

12. How do the following verses confirm God's concern with the heart?

> Matthew 5:8
>
> Matthew 5:28
>
> Matthew 6:21
>
> Matthew 15:8-9
>
> Matthew 23:25, 27

13. Parents are to train and discipline their children in love. List the characteristics of love found in 1 Corinthians 13:4-7.

14. Write your own prayer based on Galatians 6:9.

Application

1. What did you learn most from chapters three and four?

2. How did you apply this to your life this week?

3. What were the results?

Discussion Notes:

Prayer Requests:

Week Three

What causes a child to speak such tender words as "I love you" and "You're the best mommy in the world" in one breath, then in the next say something terrible? Matthew explains that it is "out of the overflow of the heart the mouth speaks" (Matthew 12:34b). In other words, there is merit to the old saying, "What's down in the well comes up in the bucket." A child's sin does not begin with his mouth; it begins with his heart. It is not sinful words that defile the heart, but a defiled heart that brings forth sinful words. An impure heart pumps sin, infects the body and spews contaminated words from the mouth. While the words our children speak alert us to a problem, we must understand that the heart is where the words are born. When the truth of God's Word reaches the heart, the tongue will take care of itself.

Reading

Chapter Five: Taming the Tongue

Chapter Six: The Power of God's Word

Memorization

Hebrews 4:12

For the word of God is alive and active. Sharper than any double-edged sword, it penetrates even to dividing soul and spirit, joints and marrow; it judges the thoughts and attitudes of the heart.

Questions: Chapter Five

1. The Bible likens the tongue to a fire with the potential to destroy. However, when used properly, what good can potentially come from the tongue?

2. What might the "unwholesome talk" mentioned in Ephesians 4:29 sound like coming from a mother?

3. What is a reproof?

4. If we fail to balance discipline and instruction, what will happen according to Ephesians 6:4?

5. What is the purpose of discipline?

6. List three negative results of chastising children for doing wrong without following through by training them in what is right.

   (1)

   (2)

   (3)

7. What must we use for teaching, rebuking, correcting and training in righteousness? Why?

8. During child-training, J.C. Ryle encourages parents to ask what question?

9. What does teaching in the "context of the moment" mean?

10. List four benefits of teaching in the "context of the moment."

   (1)

   (2)

   (3)

   (4)

11. Give a personal or hypothetical example of teaching in the context of the moment.

12. How might the law of the harvest encourage parents in child-training?

13. Based on Paul's instructions to Timothy found in 1 Timothy 4:7-8, how might a child benefit from practicing the biblical alternative to sinful behavior?

14. Explain how the apprenticeship described in chapter five provides parents with a good example for training children in godliness.

15. What do the following verses say about the manner in which our words are spoken?

> Proverbs 10:19

> Proverbs 16:21

> Proverbs 17:27

> Proverbs 29:20

> Ecclesiastes 6:11

> Ecclesiastes 9:17

16. According to Matthew 15:18, where should we begin the process of taming our own tongues as well as the tongues of our children?

Questions: Chapter Six

1. What does God use to convict his children?

2. Teaching children God's Word points them to their need for what?

3. We may view having to address certain behaviors over and over as a burden or a trial. According to James 1:2-4, what is an appropriate response to trials?

4. What is the reason children and adults sin?

5. When children sin, what choices of response do parents have?

6. We must be faithful to point our children to their need for Christ, but who alone brings about conviction and change of heart?

7. List six parental responsibilities.

    (1)

    (2)

    (3)

    (4)

    (5)

    (6)

8. In what way can parental responsibility be compared to the position of John the Baptist?

9. Read 1 Timothy 4:12. In what five areas did Paul encourage Timothy to be an example?

    (1)

    (2)

    (3)

    (4)

(5)

10. Children often follow the example parents set. What kind of example are you setting? List three good examples and three that need work.

11. Why must parents reprove their children?

12. When must parents reprove their children?

13. In what types of situations should a reproof alone be given?

14. Explain how the following verses express the importance of using God's Word for training children.

    Galatians 3:24

    2 Timothy 3:16

    Hebrews 4:12

15. In what type of situations might it be beneficial to review expectations ahead of time?

16. As instructed by Paul in Romans 12:1-2, what are the three things we need to do in order to know God's will for our lives, whether it be for training our children or anything else?

    (1)

    (2)

    (3)

Application

1. What did you learn most from chapters five and six?

2. How did you apply this to your life this week?

3. What were the results?

Discussion Notes:

Prayer Requests:

Week Four

It's late at night when you hear a ruckus coming from the kitchen. It sounds much like the popping of the glass cookie jar lid. You suspiciously tip toe to the crime scene then barge in through the swinging door. Your wide-eyed little "dear" looks as if he has been caught in the headlights. He's caught all right, but his quick and clever antics reach way beyond that of a typical three-year-old. As you temporarily experience the loss of common sense, you firmly ask, "What are you doing, son?" His chubby little arm extends, offering you the cookie as he sweetly replies, "I was getting a cookie for you, mommy ... may I have one, too?" It's easy to mistake a manipulative motive when it is clothed in clever wording combined with plain old cuteness. What's a poor mom to do? Pray for wisdom to recognize manipulation for what it is, ask God for wisdom to rightly address it and trust him to work in the heart of you and your child.

Reading

> **Chapter Seven: Managing the Manipulator**
>
> **Chapter Eight: Guidelines for Verbal Correction**

Memorization

> James 1:19-20

My dear brothers and sisters, take note of this: Everyone should be quick to listen, slow to speak and slow to become angry, because human anger does not produce the righteousness that God desires.

Questions: Chapter Seven

1. How does author Lou Priolo define manipulation?

2. List several possible tactics of a young manipulator.

3. How might a parent respond foolishly to a young manipulator?

4. How might a parent respond wisely to a young manipulator?

5. List several possible tactics of an older manipulator.

6. How might a parent respond foolishly to an older manipulator?

7. How might a parent respond wisely to an older manipulator?

8. Proverbs 26:4-5 offers instructions for responding to foolishness. Explain these verses in your own words as they would apply in parenting.

9. How did Jesus respond to manipulation?

10. As parents, we can not judge the thoughts and motives of our children, but what can we help our children do?

11. Begin watching for times when your children are attempting to manipulate. Record the instance, the tactic used and your response. Consider whether or not you responded wisely. If necessary, record how you might improve your method of response for future situations.

Questions: Chapter Eight

1. List six guidelines given for verbal correction.

    1.

    2.

    3.

    4.

    5.

    6.

2. Which of the six guidelines is your greatest strength (you may have more than one)?

3. Which of the six guidelines is your greatest weakness (you may have more than one)?

4. What good news does the gospel hold for our weaknesses according to 2 Corinthians 12:9?

5. What steps are you willing to take in order to overcome your weakness(es)?

6. If your motives are questionable, what must you do prior to disciplining your child?

7. What are the risks of correcting your child in front of others?

8. Why, in light of Hebrews 4:12, are God's Words more powerful and effective than our words?

9. List examples of worldly terminology versus biblical terminology.

10. In your own words, describe how Proverbs 15:28 offers wisdom for parents.

11. What is scolding? Is it ever appropriate to scold?

12. In addition to training our children what to "put off", we must also train them in what to "put on". Why are both important?

13. Give a personal or hypothetical scenario to demonstrate how the "put off" and "put on" principle works?

14. When is anger sinful?

15. When anger is not dealt with biblically, what can it lead to?

16. List a few ways in which sinful anger might manifest itself.

17. The *Wise Words for Moms* chart was designed to aid parents in applying Scriptures in training their children. However, we

must constantly be learning and applying Scriptures to our own lives as well. Write the following verses:

Deuteronomy 6:6

Psalm 27:1

Psalm 119:11

NOTE: The *Wise Words for Moms* chart shown at the end of chapter eight is merely a sample. The complete chart offers biblical solutions for twenty-two behaviors, such as disobeying, lying, tattling, etc.

Application

1. What did you learn most from chapters seven and eight?

2. How did you apply this to your life this week?

3. What were the results?

Discussion Notes:

Prayer Requests:

Week Five

Spanking has become extremely controversial. The most prominent argument against it being that it promotes violence in children. Yet, as parents have moved further and further away from the biblical model of spanking, children have become more and more violent. While spanking in anger is extremely likely to provoke anger in children, spanking with self-control and a motive of love is biblical, right and beneficial. When parents embrace a biblical model for disciplining their children, God is honored and working. However, it is better to refrain from spanking altogether if it cannot be done with self-control and love. Parents, who, for various reasons, cannot spank their children, might also find encouragement in remembering that spanking is only a small part of discipline.

Reading

Chapter Nine: The Tailbone's Connected to the ... Heart

Chapter Ten: The Biblical Model Works

Appendix C

Memorization

James 1:19-20

My dear brothers and sisters, take note of this: Everyone should be quick to listen, slow to speak and slow to become angry, because human anger does not produce the righteousness that God desires.

Questions: Chapter Nine

1. Under what circumstances would it be better for a parent to refrain from spanking?

2. What can a worldly and non-biblical use of the rod lead to?

3. Write Tedd Tripp's definition of the rod.

4. How do the following verses warn against worldly wisdom?

　　1 Corinthians 3:18-19

　　Colossians 2:8

5. Craft your own definition of the word "careful" as it is used in Proverbs 13:24

6. What should motivate a parent to use the rod?

7. What practical wisdom do the following verses offer when applied to child-training?

　　Proverbs 15:28

　　James 1:19-20

8. When training is done properly, how should it end?

9. When parents make excuses for their children's sinful behavior, what negative message are they instilling?

10. When parents take the time necessary to properly train and discipline their children, what positive message are they instilling?

11. How might Hebrews 12:5-7 and 10-12 encourage children to willingly receive discipline?

12. According to Proverbs 5:12-14, what happens to the person who despises discipline?

13. Read Proverbs 11:18. Contrast what happens to those who choose wickedness with those who choose righteousness.

14. Why, as stated in Deuteronomy 32:45-47, must we take to heart the Word of God?

Questions: Chapter Ten

1. List three reasons parents are called to use the rod.

   1)

   2)

   3)

2. What are a few common excuses parents make for not using the rod?

3. When are children old enough to learn "no" and to be trained to obey?

4. Our hope, wisdom, strength and joy in parenting are found in Christ alone. How do the following verses express this truth?

   2 Chronicles 7:14

   Isaiah 41:10

   John 15:4-5

5. When spankings seem to be ineffective, list four possible reasons why.

   1)

   2)

   3)

   4)

6. Explain how children have more freedom through boundaries.

7. How do boundaries help establish security in children?

8. How can discipline that is based on the energy level, mood or whim of the parent affect a child in negative ways?

9. According to Hebrews 12:11, what and when do we reap?

10. List two or more sinful motives for disciplining a child.

11. Our primary goal in parenting should be to point our children to Christ through the good news of the gospel. Read Psalm 145:4-7 and list the ways a parent might commend the works of God.

12. Look up Galatians 6:9. How does this verse encourage you in parenting?

Application

1. What did you learn most from chapters five and six?

2. How did you apply this to your life this week?

3. What were the results?

Discussion Notes:

Prayer Requests:

Week Six

When we set standards of obedience for our children and do not follow through with consequences when those standards are violated, we send our children mixed signals. This is not only confusing and unfair, but also teaches them that we are not people of our word, which evokes a lack of trust in the parent/child relationship. Standards are useless without consistency. We must say what we mean and mean what we say, even during moments when it is inconvenient to do so. We set standards of obedience because we love our children and desire what is best for them. We know that when they learn to obey us, they are becoming better equipped to obey God, which is our ultimate goal.

Reading

> **Chapter Eleven:** Setting the Standard for
>   Obedience
>
> **Chapter Twelve:** To Spank or not to Spank

Memorization

Galatians 6:9

Let us not become weary in doing good, for at the proper time we will reap a harvest if we do not give up.

Questions: Chapter Eleven

1. Describe biblical obedience.

2. Read 1 Samuel 15. What excuses did Saul make for his disobedience?

3. What was the consequence for Saul's disobedience?

4. Is delayed obedience acceptable? Why or why not?

5. How can allowing delayed obedience confuse and/or frustrate children?

6. Explain how attitudes are issues of the will, not the emotions.

7. In the verses below, what commands are given to help us acquire right attitudes?

   (a) Philippians 2:14

   (b) 1 Thessalonians 5:16-18

8. List a few traps parents fall into in an attempt to gain obedience and why they should be avoided.

9. How might a child benefit spiritually from learning to habitually obey his or her parents?

10. Why is it important to be consistent in disciplining even the small acts of disobedience?

11. When parents allow disobedience, who are parents disobeying?

12. What steps might a disobedient parent take in order to get back on the right track?

13. How can indulging a "tea pot" temper lead a parent to sin against God and her child?

14. On whom must a parent who is prone to a "tea pot" temper depend?

Questions: Chapter Twelve

1. List a few situations where it would be inappropriate to spank.

2. When does childishness transition into foolishness?

3. Parents should encourage their children to acknowledge God in everything. According to Romans 1:28, what can happen when God's authority is repeatedly rebelled against?

4. If a parent is angry, what must that parent do before administering discipline?

5. The rod is useful and appropriate for correcting what two areas of foolishness?

    1)

    2)

6. List nine guidelines for spanking.

    1)

    2)

    3)

    4)

    5)

    6)

    7)

    8)

    9)

7. In what ways did Jesus exemplify true forgiveness?

8. What does it mean to make restitution? Give an example.

9. Is it ever too late to begin training children?

10. Read Hebrews 3:12-13 and answer the following questions:

    1) What is the warning / danger stated in this passage?

    2) What are we to do to help avoid this danger?

11. According to Galatians 6:1, how are we to restore someone who is caught in sin? If we are not careful, what sort of temptations might *we* succumb to?

12. Children learn by the example set by the parents. How does Ephesians 5:15-17 say we are to live?

13. Write Proverbs 3:5-6 in the space below.

14. We may become discouraged at times and think that it is no use, but our responsibility in training our children is to trust God, do what he says and leave the results to him. How does this change your thinking?

Application

1. What did you learn most from chapters eleven and twelve?

2. How did you apply this to your life this week?

3. What were the results?

Discussion Notes:

Prayer Requests: